THE BEATLES

ISBN 978-1-70518-815-6

Visit Hal Leonard Online at
www.halleonard.com

World headquarters, contact:
Hal Leonard
7777 West Bluemound Road
Milwaukee, WI 53213
Email: info@halleonard.com

In Europe, contact:
Hal Leonard Europe Limited
1 Red Place
London, W1K 6PL
Email: info@halleonardeurope.com

In Australia, contact:
Hal Leonard Australia Pty. Ltd.
4 Lentara Court
Cheltenham, Victoria, 3192 Australia
Email: info@halleonard.com.au

ALL MY LOVING

Words and Music by JOHN LENNON
and PAUL McCARTNEY

Moderately fast

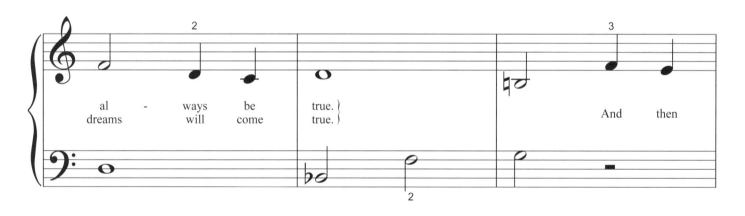

day, _____ and I'll send all my lov - ing to

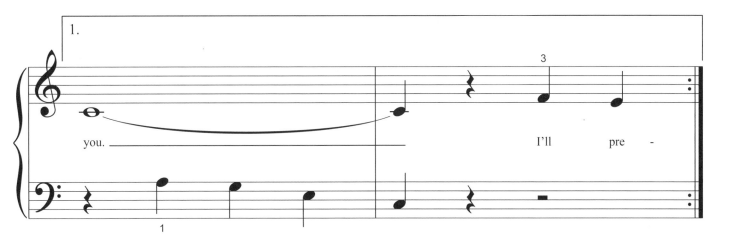

1.

you. _____ I'll pre -

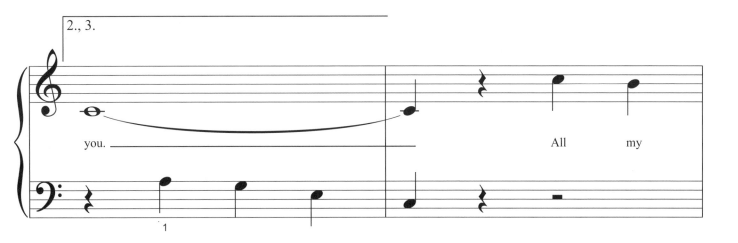

2., 3.

you. _____ All my

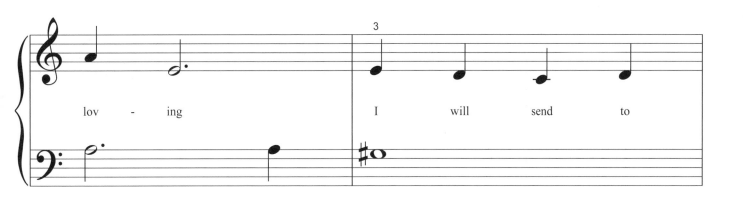

lov - ing I will send to

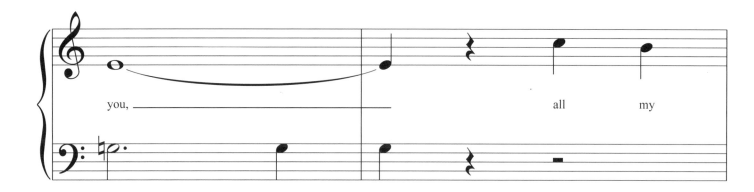

you, _____ _____ all my

To Coda

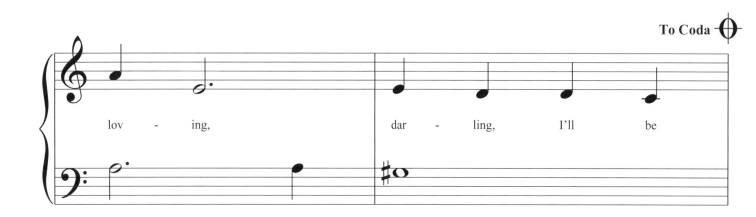

lov - ing, dar - ling, I'll be

D.S. al Coda
(verse 1, no repeat)

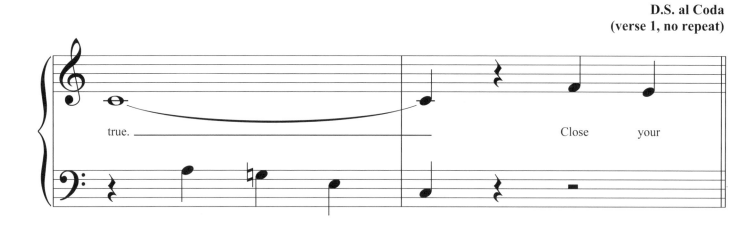

true. _____ Close your

CODA

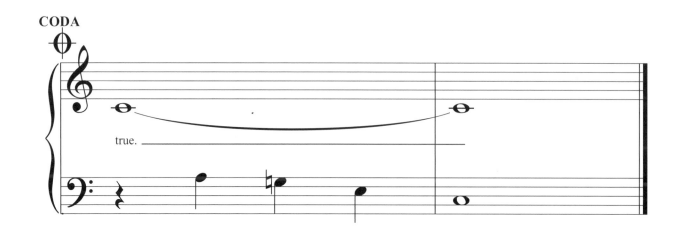

true. _____

EIGHT DAYS A WEEK

Words and Music by JOHN LENNON
and PAUL McCARTNEY

love me, _____ I ain't got noth - in' but

To Coda ⊕

love babe, _____ eight days a

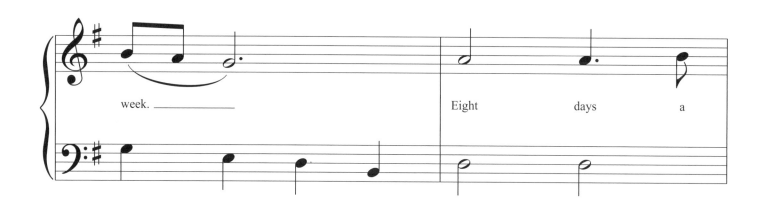

week. _____ Eight days a

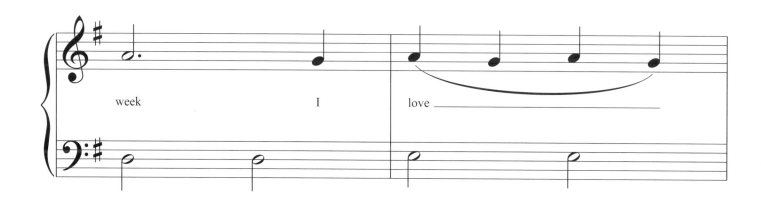

week I love _____

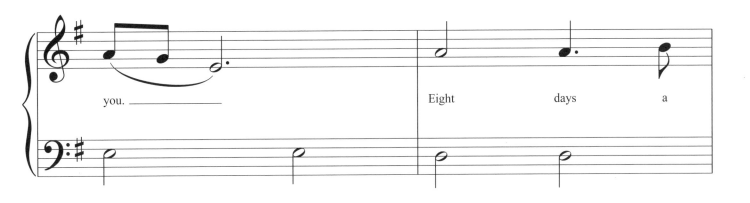

you. _____ Eight days a

D.C. al Coda

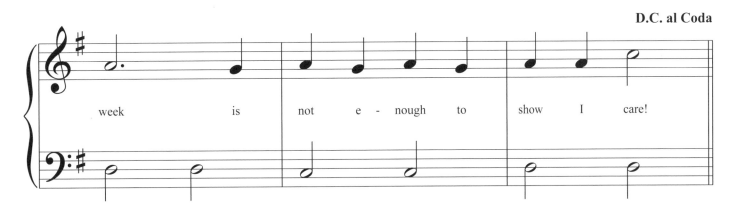

week ___ is ___ not e - nough to ___ show I care!

CODA

week. _____ Eight days a

week, _____ eight days a week. _____

All You Need Is Love

Words and Music by JOHN LENNON
and PAUL McCARTNEY

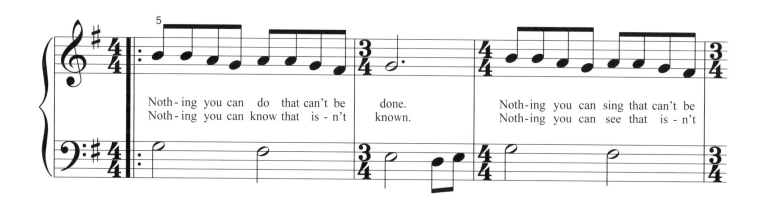

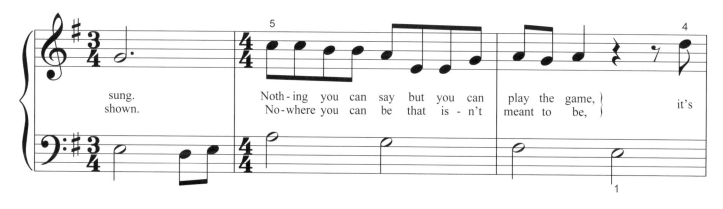

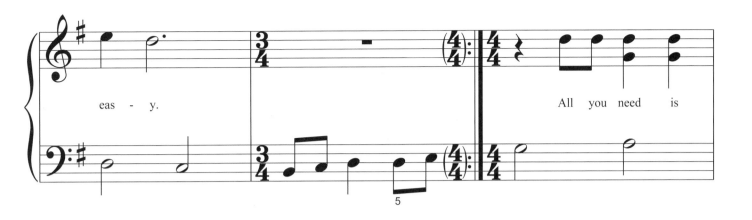

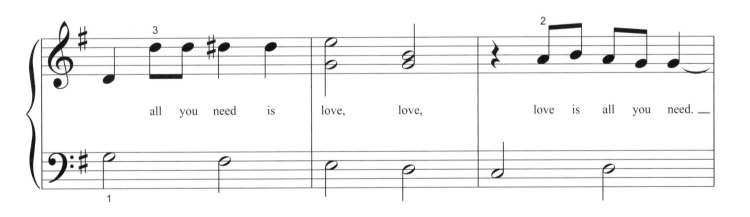

CAN'T BUY ME LOVE

Words and Music by JOHN LENNON
and PAUL McCARTNEY

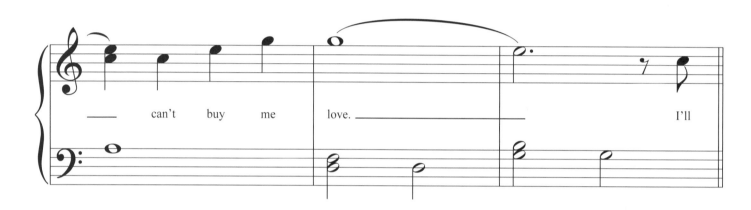

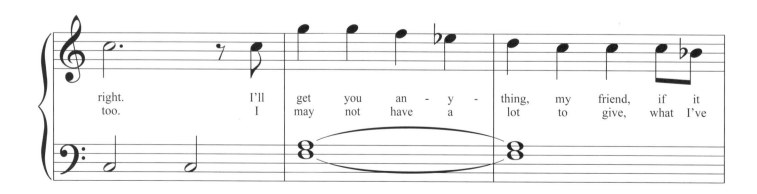

makes   you   feel   al - right.
got   I'll   give   to   you.   'Cause   I   don't   care   too

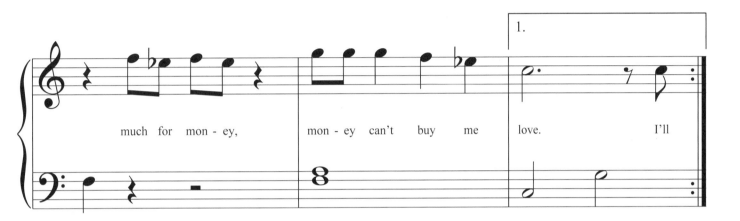

much   for   mon - ey,   mon - ey   can't   buy   me   love.   I'll

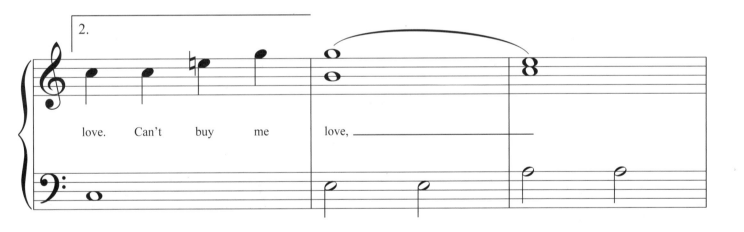

love.   Can't   buy   me   love,

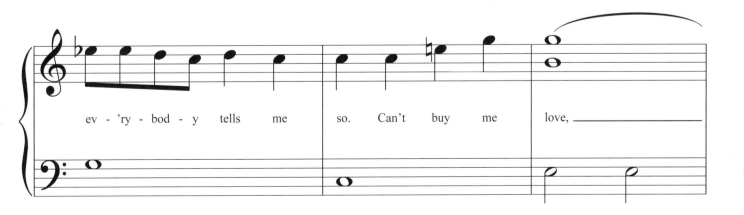

ev - 'ry - bod - y   tells   me   so.   Can't   buy   me   love,

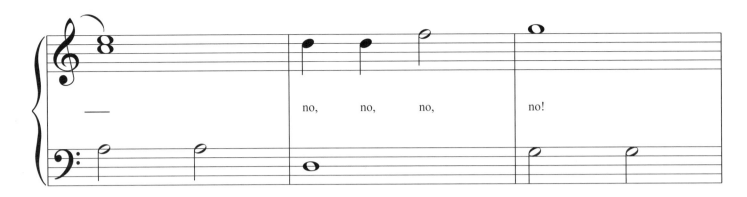

no, no, no, no!

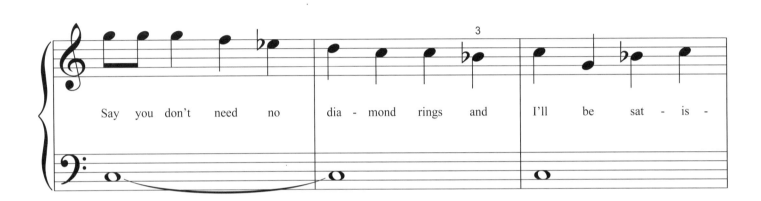

Say you don't need no dia - mond rings and I'll be sat - is -

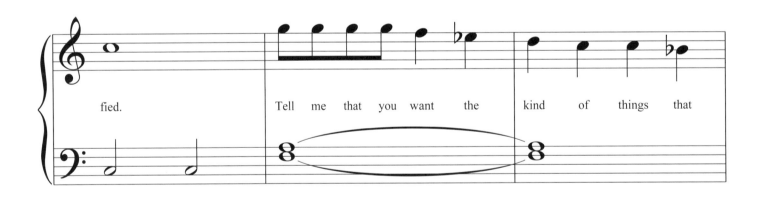

fied. Tell me that you want the kind of things that

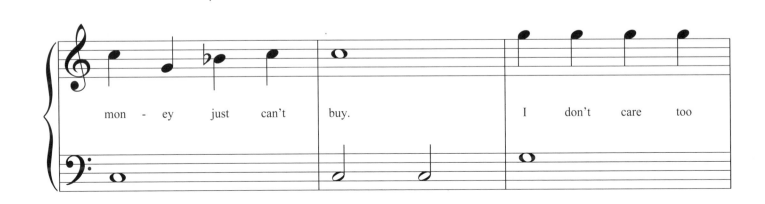

mon - ey just can't buy. I don't care too

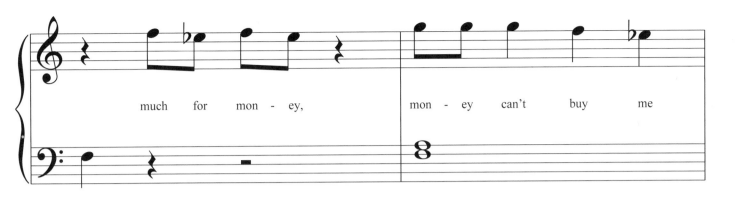

much   for   mon - ey,   mon - ey   can't   buy   me

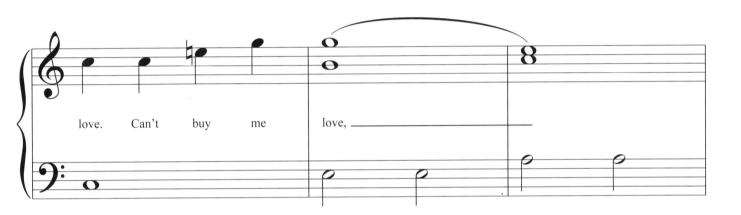

love.   Can't   buy   me   love, _____

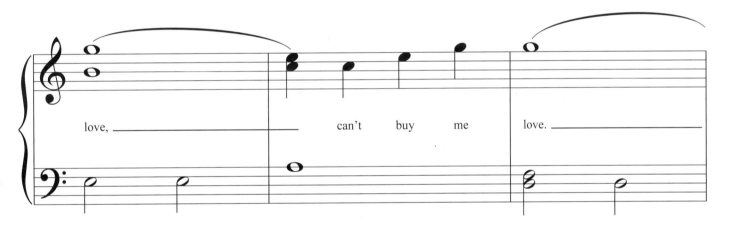

love, _____   can't   buy   me   love. _____

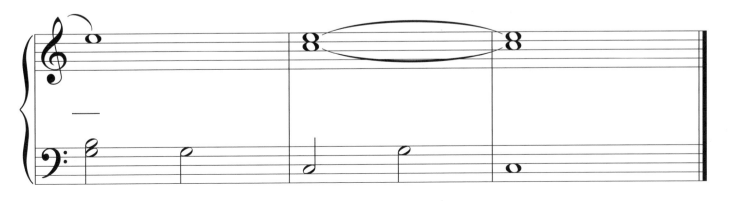

ELEANOR RIGBY

Words and Music by JOHN LENNON
and PAUL McCARTNEY

Moderately fast

Ah,   look at all   the lone - ly   peo - ple!

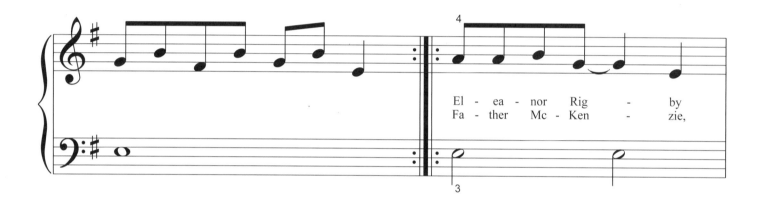

El - ea - nor Rig -   by
Fa - ther Mc - Ken -   zie,

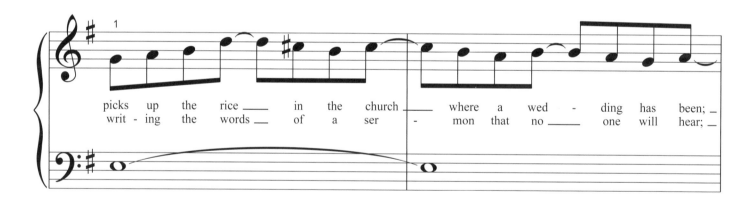

picks up the rice ____ in the church ____ where a wed - ding has been; ___
writ - ing the words ____ of a ser - mon that no ____ one will hear; ___

____ lives in a dream. _____ Waits at the win - dow,
no one comes near. _____ Look at him work - ing,

wear - ing the face ____ that she keeps ____ in a jar ____ by the door; _
darn - ing his socks ____ in the night ____ when there's no - bod - y there; _

____ who is it for? ____ } All the lone - ly peo - ple, where
what does he care? ____

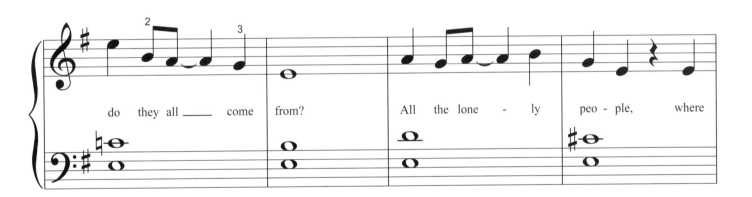

do they all ____ come from? All the lone - ly peo - ple, where

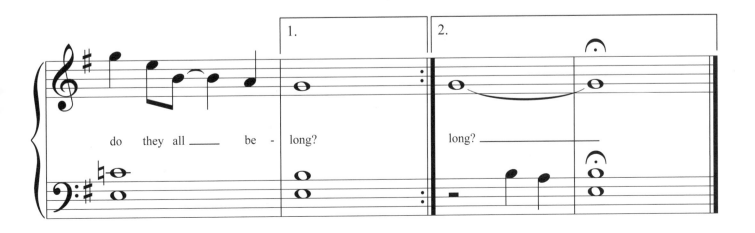

1.
do they all ____ be - long?

2.
long? ____

HEY JUDE

Words and Music by JOHN LENNON
and PAUL McCARTNEY

Jude, _____ don't be a - fraid; you were
Jude, _____ don't let me down; you have

made to _____ go out and get her. _____ The
found her, _____ now go and get her. _____ Re -

min - ute you let her un - der your skin, then you be - gin ___
mem - ber to let her in - to your heart, then you can start ___

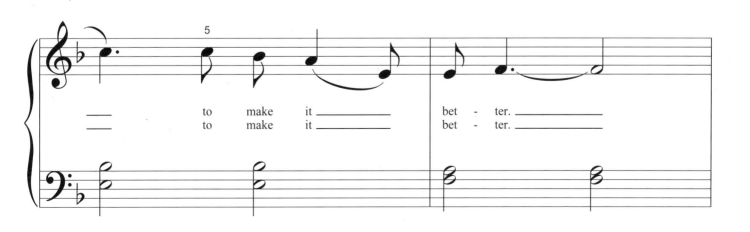

___ to make it _____ bet - ter. _____
___ to make it _____ bet - ter. _____

18

And an - y - time you feel the pain, hey Jude, _____ re -
So let it out and let it in, hey Jude, _____ be -

frain; don't car - ry the world up - on _____ your
gin; you're wait - ing for some - one to _____ per -

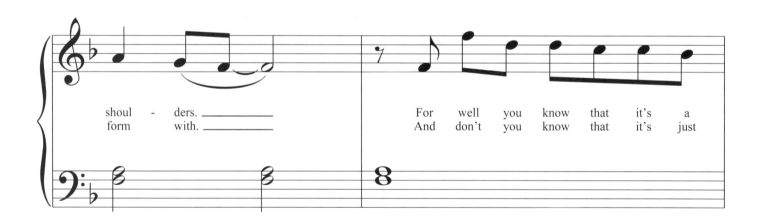

shoul - ders. _____
form with. _____

For well you know that it's a
And don't you know that it's just

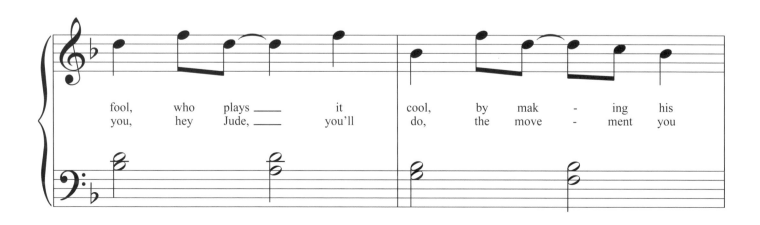

fool, who plays _____ it cool, by mak - ing his
you, hey Jude, _____ you'll do, the move - ment you

mem - ber   to   let   her   un - der   your   skin,   then   you'll   be - gin ___

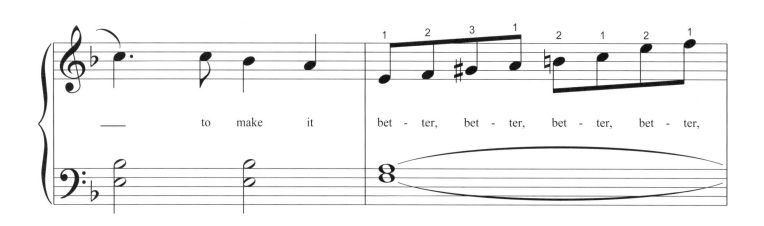

___   to   make   it   bet - ter,   bet - ter,   bet - ter,   bet - ter,

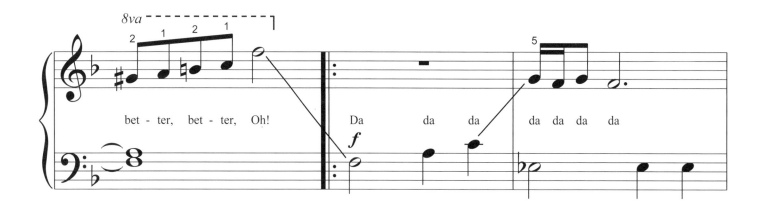

bet - ter,   bet - ter,   Oh!   Da   da   da   da   da   da   da

Repeat and Fade | **Optional Ending**

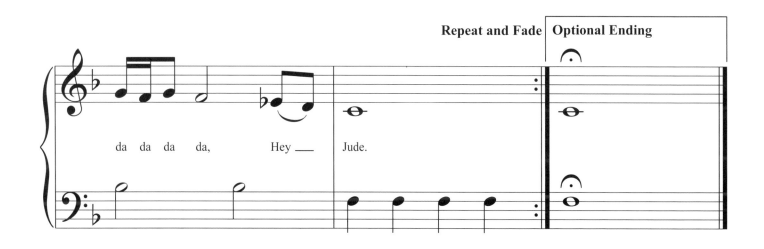

da   da   da   da,   Hey ___   Jude.

Here, There AND Everywhere

Words and Music by JOHN LENNON
and PAUL McCARTNEY

ev - ry - where   and   if   she's   be - side   me   I   know   I   need

nev - er   care.   But   to   love   her   is   to   meet   her

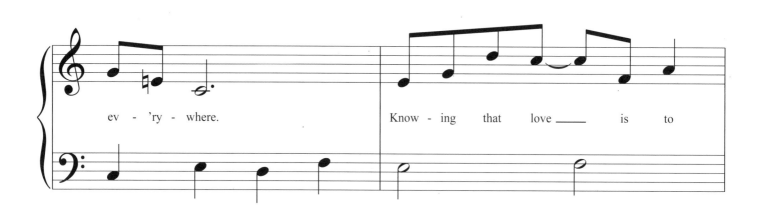

ev - 'ry - where.   Know - ing   that   love _____   is   to

share,   each   one   be - lieve - ing   that

love nev - er dies, _____ watch - ing her eyes _____ and

1.

hop - ing I'm al - ways there. I want her

2.

there to be there, and ev - 'ry - where.

2

Here, there, and ev - 'ry - where. _____

I AM THE WALRUS

Words and Music by JOHN LENNON
and PAUL McCARTNEY

Cor-por - a - tion tee shirt, stu-pid blood-y Tues-day man, you been a naugh-ty boy, you let your face grow

long.   I am the egg - man,   they are the

egg - man,   I am the wal - rus.   Goo goo g' joob.

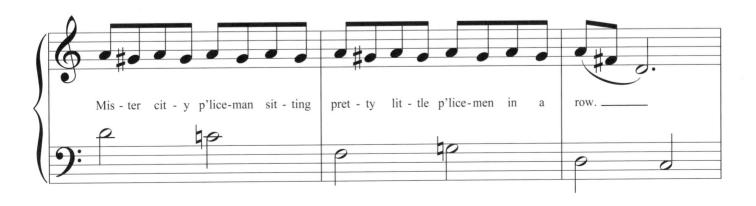

Mis - ter cit - y p'lice-man sit - ting pret - ty lit - tle p'lice-men in a row. _____

See how they fly, like Lu - cy in the sky, see how ___ they run. ___ I'm

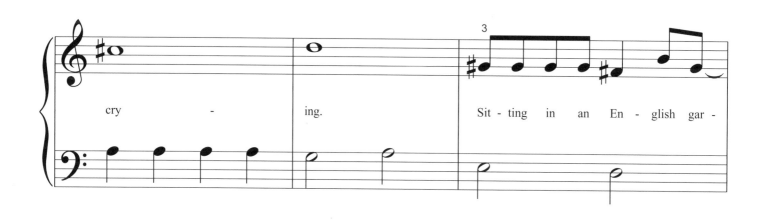

cry - ing. I'm cry - ing. I'm

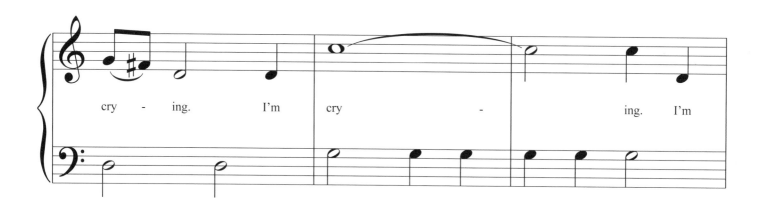

cry - ing. Sit - ting in an En - glish gar -

- den wait - ing for the sun. ___ If the sun don't

come, you get a tan from stand-ing in the En - glish rain.   I am the

egg - man.   They are the   egg - man.   I am the

wal - rus.   Goo goo g' joob g'   goo goo g' joob.

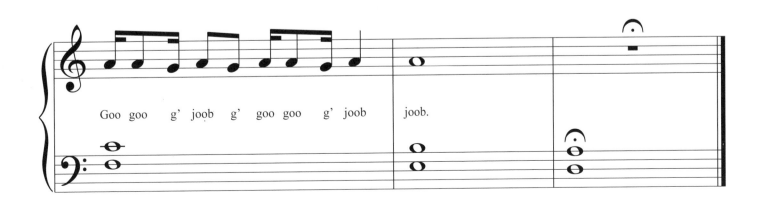

Goo goo g' joob g' goo goo g' joob   joob.

IN MY LIFE

Words and Music by JOHN LENNON
and PAUL McCARTNEY

Moderately

There are plac - es I re - mem - ber, all my
all these friends and lov - ers, there is

mp

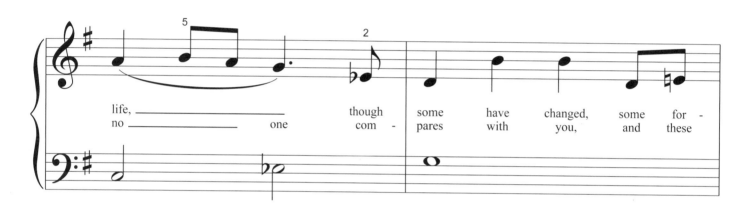

life, _____ though some have changed, some for -
no _____ one com - pares with you, and these

ev - er, not for bet - ter, some have gone _____ and
mem - 'ries lose their mean - ing when I think of _____ love and as

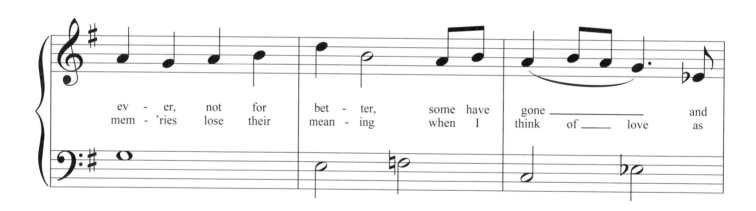

some re - main. All those plac - es _____ had _____ their _____ mo - ments with
some - thing new. Though I know _____ I'll _____ nev - er lose af - fec - tion for

lov - ers and friends ___ I
peo - ple and things ___ that

still can re - call. ___ Some are
went ___ be - fore, ___ I

dead ___ and ___ some ___ are ___ liv - ing. In my ___ life, I've
know I'll of - ten stop and think a - bout them. In my ___ life, I

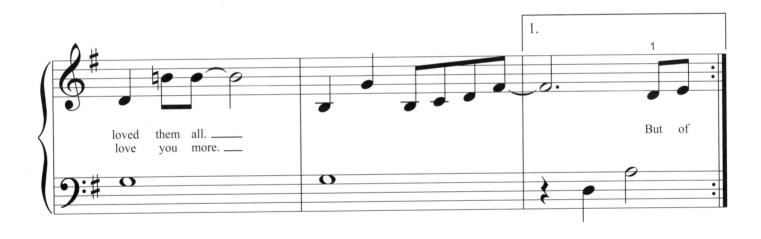

1.

loved them all. ___
love you more. ___

But of

2.

LET IT BE

Words and Music by JOHN LENNON
and PAUL McCARTNEY

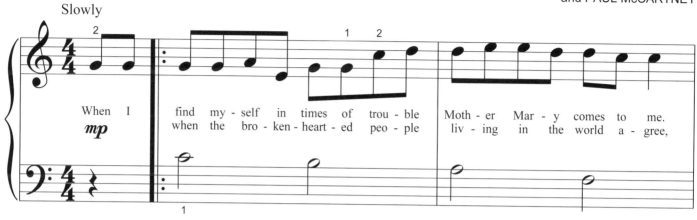

Slowly

When I find my-self in times of trou-ble Moth-er Mar-y comes to me.
when the bro-ken-heart-ed peo-ple liv-ing in the world a-gree,

Speak-ing words of wis-dom, let it be. _____ And in my hour of dark-ness, she is
there will be an an-swer, let it be. _____ For though they may be part-ed there is

stand-ing right in front of me, speak-ing words of wis-dom, let it
still a chance that they will see, there will be an an-swer, let it

OCTOPUS'S GARDEN

Words and Music by
RICHARD STARKEY

oc - to - pus - 's   gar - den   in the   shade.
oc - to - pus - 's   gar - den   near a   cave.

I'd   ask   my   friends   to
We would   sing   and

come   and   see _____   an oc - to -
dance a - round _____   be - cause we

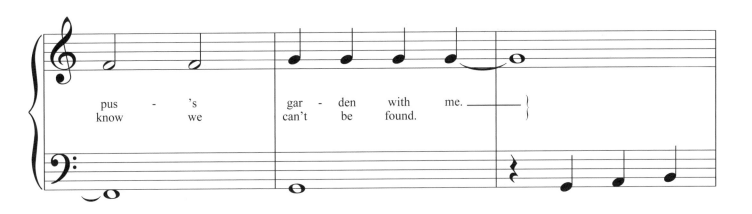

pus - 's   gar - den with me. _____
know we   can't be found.

I'd like to be ___ un - der the sea ___

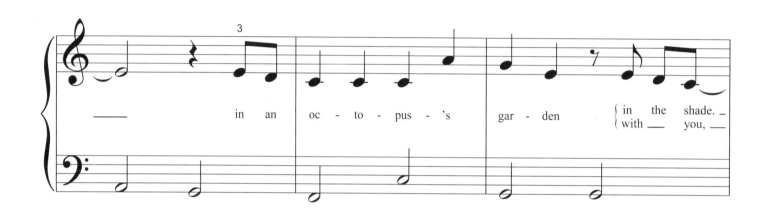

___ in an oc - to - pus - 's gar - den { in the shade. ___ with ___ you, ___

1.

2.

in an oc - to - pus - 's

gar - den with you.

PENNY LANE

Words and Music by JOHN LENNON
and PAUL McCARTNEY

Pen - ny Lane: There is a bar - ber show - ing pho - to - graphs of ev - 'ry

head he's had the plea - sure to know, _____ and all the peo - ple that come and

go stop and say hel - lo. On the

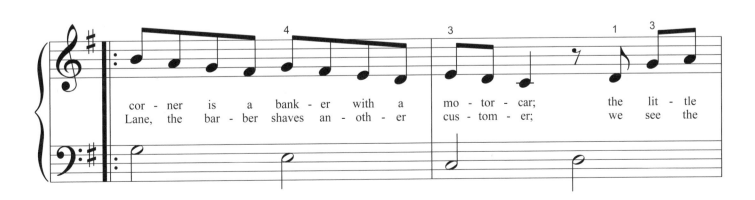

cor - ner is a bank - er with a mo - tor - car; the lit - tle
Lane, the bar - ber shaves an - oth - er cus - tom - er; we see the

chil - dren laugh at him be - hind his back. And the
bank - er sit - ting wait - ing for a trim. And the

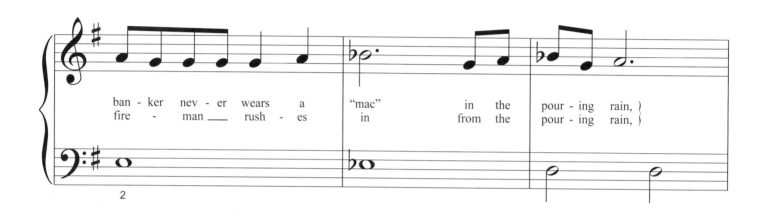

ban - ker nev - er wears a "mac" in the pour - ing rain,)
fire - man ___ rush - es in from the pour - ing rain,)

ver - y strange! Pen - ny Lane is in my ears and in my

eyes, ___ there be - neath the

blue sub - ur - ban skies I sit. And mean - while, back in Pen - ny

mean - while, back... Pen - ny Lane is in my ears and in my

eyes, _____ there be - neath the

blue sub - ur - ban skies, Pen - ny Lane. _____

SOMETHING

Words and Music by
GEORGE HARRISON

Moderately slow

Some - thing in the way she moves
Some - thing in her smile she knows

mf

at - tracts me like no oth - er lov - er,
that I don't need no oth - er lov - er,

some - thing in the way she woos ____ me }
some - thing in her style she that shows ____ me }   I

don't want to leave _____ her now, you

3rd time To Coda

know I be - lieve ___ and how. ___

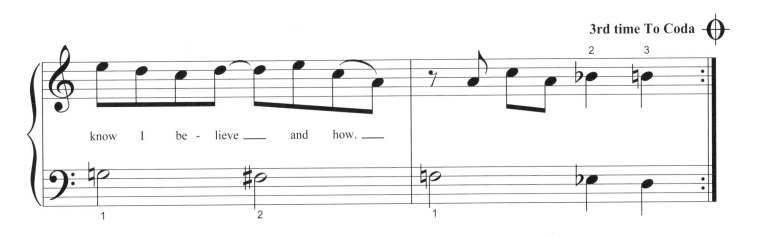

You're ask - ing me will my love

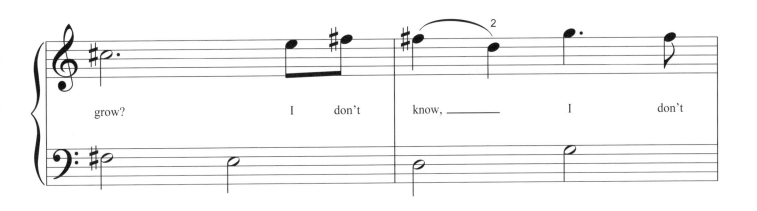

grow? I don't know, _____ I don't

know.

You stick a - round now, it may

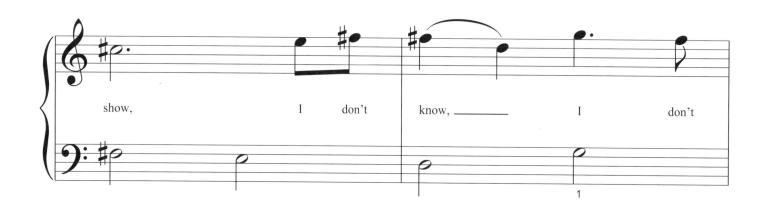

show,   I don't   know, _____   I   don't

D.C. al Coda
(without repeat)

CODA

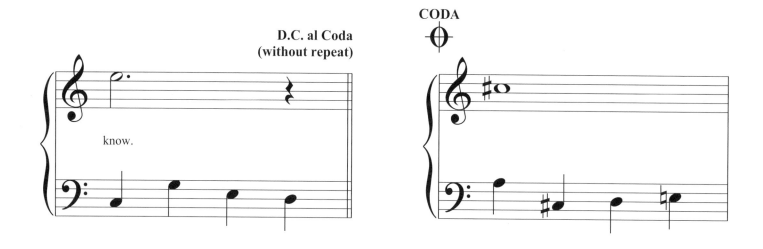

know.

WITH A LITTLE HELP FROM MY FRIENDS

Words and Music by JOHN LENNON
and PAUL McCARTNEY

42

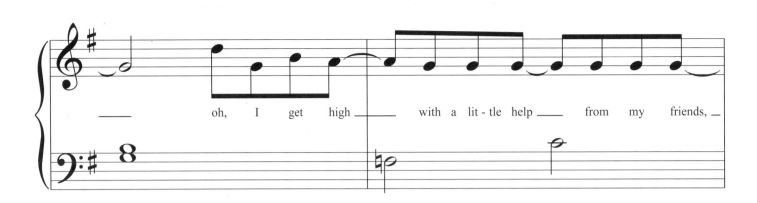

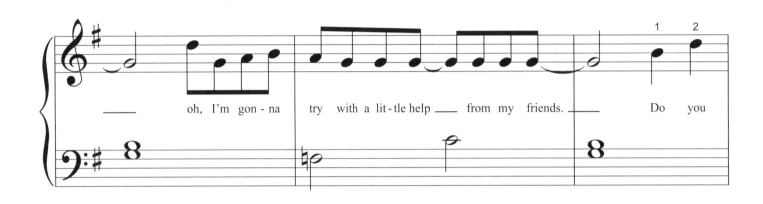

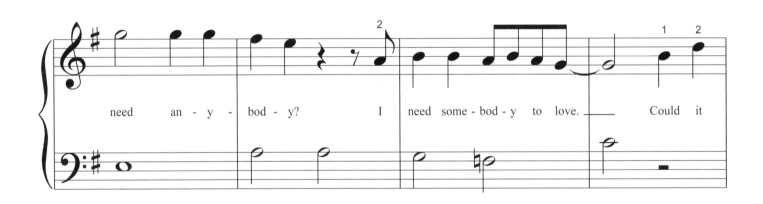

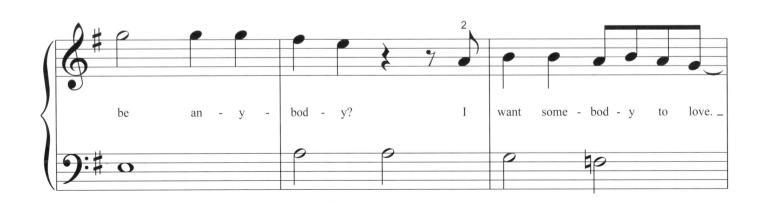

Oh, I get by _____ with a lit-tle help _____ from my friends, _____ oh, I'm gon - na

try with a lit - tle help _____ from my friends. _____ Yes, I get high _____

_____ with a lit-tle help _____ from my friends, _____ with a lit - tle help _____ from my

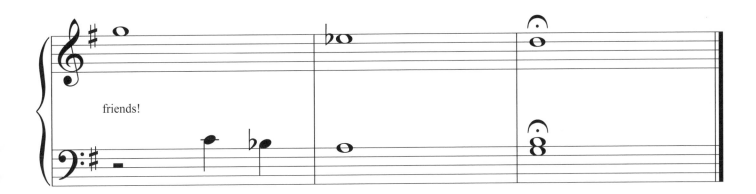

friends!

STRAWBERRY FIELDS FOREVER

Words and Music by JOHN LENNON
and PAUL McCARTNEY

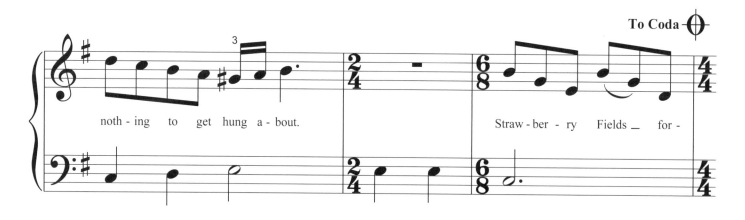

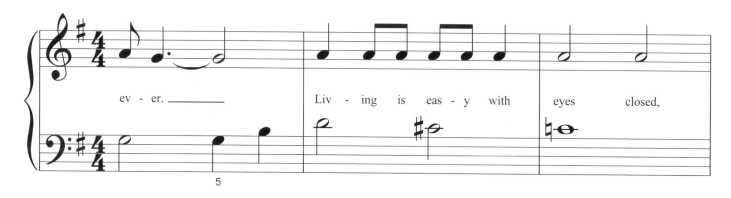

mis - un - der - stand - ing all you see. ____ It's get - ting hard to be some-

D.C. al Coda

one, but it all works out; it does-n't mat - ter much to me.

CODA

ev - er. ____ Straw-ber - ry Fields _ for - ev - er. ____

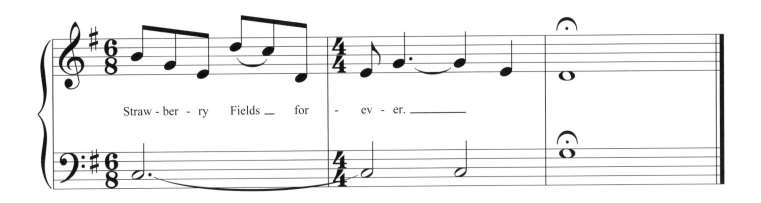

Straw - ber - ry Fields _ for - ev - er. _____

YESTERDAY

Words and Music by JOHN LENNON
and PAUL McCARTNEY

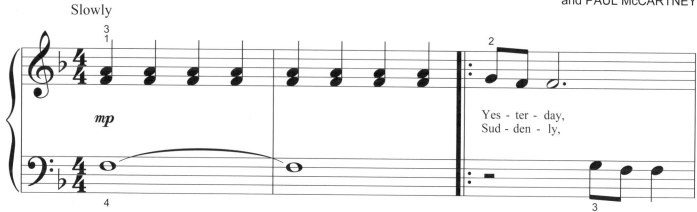

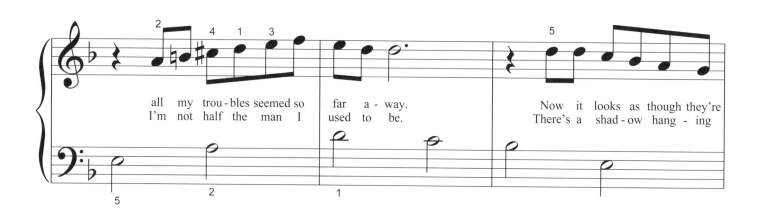

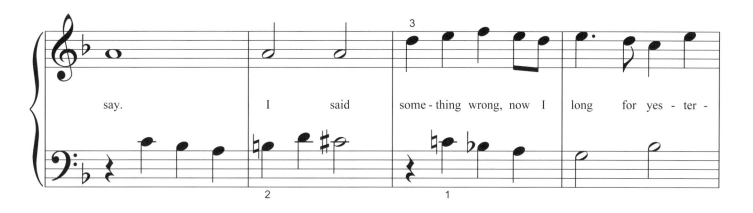

say.   I   said   some - thing wrong, now I   long   for yes - ter -

day.   Yes - ter - day,   love was such an eas - y

game to play.   Now I need a place to   hide a - way.   Oh,

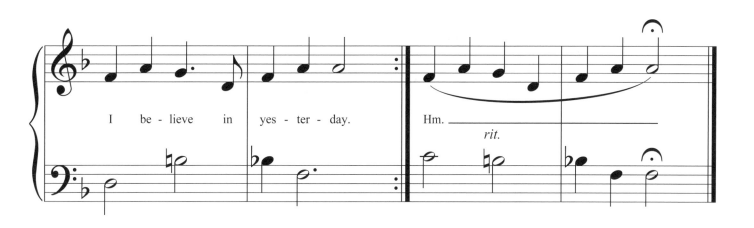

I be - lieve in   yes - ter - day.   Hm. _____   *rit.*